THE CUBAN MISSILE CRISIS

Essential Events

THE CUBAN MISSILE CRISIS

BY HELGA SCHIER

Content Consultant
Timothy McKeown, Ph.D., Professor of Political Science
University of North Carolina, Chapel Hill

ABDO
Publishing Company

CREDITS

Published by ABDO Publishing Company, 8000 West 78th Street, Edina, Minnesota 55439. Copyright © 2008 by Abdo Consulting Group, Inc. International copyrights reserved in all countries. No part of this book may be reproduced in any form without written permission from the publisher. The Essential Library™ is a trademark and logo of ABDO Publishing Company.

Printed in the United States.

Editor: Rebecca Rowell
Copy Editor: Paula Lewis
Interior Design and Production: Nicole Brecke
Cover Design: Becky Daum

Library of Congress Cataloging-in-Publication Data
Schier, Helga.
  The Cuban Missile Crisis / Helga Schier.
    p. cm. — (Essential events)
  Includes bibliographical references.
  ISBN 978-1-60453-046-9
  1. Cuban Missile Crisis, 1962—Juvenile literature. I. Title.

E841.S295 2008
972.9106′4—dc22

                          2007031209

TABLE OF CONTENTS

MISSILE ERECTOR

THEODOLITE STATION

CABLE

5 TRUCKS UNDER CAMOUFLAGE NETTING

MISSILE SHELTER TENTS

This photograph, taken on October 23, 1962,
shows a missile site under construction in Cuba.

THE CRISIS UNFOLDS

*I*n the early morning of October 14,
1962, a U.S. spy plane flew over Cuba,
an island approximately 90 miles (145 km) south
of Florida, taking pictures of military installations.
The photographs revealed Soviet missile sites.

On October 15, National Security Advisor McGeorge Bundy was told about the photographs. The next day, he informed President John F. Kennedy.

Kennedy immediately ordered a meeting of U.S. military representatives, diplomats, and politicians. The group came to be known as the Executive Committee of the National Security Council, or Ex-Comm. These men would meet daily for the next 13 days to discuss how to handle the situation in Cuba.

At the time, the Cold War dominated U.S. foreign policy. The war divided the world into Eastern and Western blocs based on attitudes toward communism. The Eastern bloc was organized by the Soviet Union and favored communism. The Western bloc was organized by the United States and favored capitalism. Since World War II, the two sides had battled over Europe, Asia, Africa,

Ex-Comm

The Executive Committee of the National Security Council, Ex-Comm, was a group of almost two dozen U.S. officials that President Kennedy assembled to advise him during the Cuban Missile Crisis. The group met on a daily basis. Not every member attended every meeting. The discussions were tape-recorded secretly on Kennedy's orders. The group first met on October 16, 1962, but it was not officially established until October 22.

Cold War

The term "Cold War" refers to the period between 1945 and 1989 characterized by a division of the world into two groups of countries based on political allies and economic beliefs. Countries in the Eastern Bloc allied with the Soviet Union and favored communism. Countries in the Western Bloc allied with the United States and favored capitalism.

The conflict never escalated into an armed battle between the two superpowers: the Soviet Union and the United States. Instead, the two countries confronted each other in other countries' wars, such as the Korean War and the Vietnam War. They also competed economically and politically. The Cold War was marked by the looming threat of nuclear strikes and counterstrikes. The fall of the Berlin Wall in 1989 signaled the end of the Cold War.

and Latin America. Each side fought for dominance of its own political system and containment of the other side's political system. The United States and the Soviet Union engaged in an arms race aimed at amassing enough nuclear weaponry to discourage the opponent from using force. Each side threatened nuclear retaliation if the other side attacked.

Just a few weeks earlier, the Soviet Union's leader, Premier Nikita Khrushchev, had publicly stated that no offensive weapons would be stationed in Cuba. He also said that all weaponry in Cuba was meant to defend Cuba's independence and ensure the safety of Fidel Castro, Cuba's leader. However, the photographs showed the Soviet bases being readied for medium-range missiles. Soviet missiles in Cuba aimed at U.S. cities would increase Soviet striking power and decrease the warning time of Soviet attack.

DECIDING ON A RESPONSE

Kennedy's advisors interpreted the Soviet missiles in Cuba as a threat to U.S. security. The development significantly undermined the United States' advantage in the arms race and reflected poorly on the nation's image as a strong country. The situation came at a particularly bad time for the White House, as the campaign for the midterm elections in November was in full swing. Physically and politically, the presence of the Soviet missiles so close to U.S. shores simply could not be ignored.

Ex-Comm met during the evening of October 16. Marshall Carter, deputy director of the Central Intelligence Agency (CIA), warned that the missiles in Cuba might be operational within two weeks—individual missiles perhaps even sooner. It was necessary to take action quickly.

Secretary of Defense Robert McNamara presented three possible courses of action:

- ❖ Negotiate a settlement with Khrushchev.
- ❖ Declare open surveillance of military activity on the island and establish a U.S. blockade of all offensive military shipments to Cuba.
- ❖ Carry out air strikes against the missile sites, followed by an invasion of Cuba.

Secretary of Defense Robert McNamara spoke
at a news conference on October 23, 1962.

Ex-Comm members debated these options. Some members considered the first option, diplomacy, too weak a response. The United States might lose an important battle in the Cold War.

The second option, a blockade, was legally questionable because it was viewed in international law as an act of war. In addition, a blockade might prompt Soviet retaliation elsewhere, which could lead to a global nuclear war.

The third option was a large-scale military response. This might lead to a Soviet attack in Berlin, which would lead to war. Berlin had become the symbol of the division between East and West after World War II. At that time, the Allies divided the city and Germany into four sectors. Berlin was located in the section of Germany controlled by the Soviet Union. The Soviets tightly controlled their zone.

The Joint Chiefs of Staff, the leaders of the armed forces, favored the third option. However, Attorney General Robert Kennedy noted that the proposed attack seemed similar to Pearl Harbor, the Japanese attack on Hawaii that brought the United States into World War II. This time, the United States would be the aggressor, throwing its immense military might at a relatively small country. This would severely damage the United States' image.

Opinions clashed. Emotions sometimes ran high. Ex-Comm was far from reaching a consensus.

Behind Closed Doors

In September, when U.S. officials had begun to detect suspicious Soviet activity, President Kennedy ordered them to prepare plans for an air strike or a blockade. Plans involved raising military alert levels, informing the North Atlantic Treaty Organization (NATO) partners, and strengthening military presence in Florida and the U.S. military outpost in Guantanamo Bay, Cuba. Kennedy was preparing the United States for the possibility of war. Ex-Comm was trying to get the government and military ready.

On October 20, Kennedy ordered a blockade of Cuba aimed only at offensive weapons, not at food, other civilian goods, or even weapons such as rifles or machine guns. To avoid possible legal issues involved with a U.S. blockade in international waters, the term "quarantine" was used, stressing the temporary nature of the measure.

Secrecy was an important factor in the plan. On October 21, it became clear that the *New York Times* was piecing together the details of the looming crisis. Kennedy called press representatives and urged them to hold their story in order to give the United States the element of surprise. The press agreed not to break the story for 24 hours.

Going Public

On October 22, Kennedy met with congressional leaders, seeking their approval of the quarantine.

The U.S. State Department issued a message to its diplomatic corps around the world to inform foreign governments of the impending quarantine. At 6:00 p.m., Secretary of State Dean Rusk met with Soviet Ambassador to the United States Anatoly Dobrynin. Rusk presented an advance copy of the speech Kennedy was going to deliver on national television an hour later.

In his televised speech, Kennedy announced that Soviet missile sites and nuclear-capable bombers had been detected in Cuba. He stated that "the purpose of these bases can be none other than to provide a nuclear strike capability against the Western Hemisphere."[1] He demanded that they be dismantled immediately. Kennedy warned that the United States would "regard any nuclear missile launched from Cuba against any nation in the Western Hemisphere as an attack by the

Missiles in Cuba

Continued spy plane surveillance flights over Cuba found evidence of medium-range ballistic missile (MRBM) and intermediate-range ballistic missile (IRBM) sites. A ballistic missile is designed to strike a predetermined target. Its flight path is determined by the rules of ballistics, which is the study of the behavior of projectiles. An MRBM has a range of 621 to 932 miles (1,000 to 1,500 km). An IRBM has a range of 4,828 to 8,851 miles (7,770 to 14,244 km). Launched from Cuba, the IRBMs could have reached every city in the United States except for Seattle.

Soviet Union on the United States, requiring a full retaliatory response against the Soviet Union."[2]

As a first step, the United States was planning to impose a quarantine on all offensive military shipments to Cuba as of 10:00 a.m. on October 24.

As Kennedy delivered his speech, U.S. military forces worldwide went to DEFCON 3, an increased alert status. U.S. Navy vessels headed toward the quarantine line, armed with nuclear warheads. B-52 bombers armed with nuclear weapons began

John F. Kennedy

John Fitzgerald Kennedy was born into a wealthy political family on May 29, 1917, in Brookline, Massachusetts. After graduating from Harvard in 1940, Kennedy served as a naval officer during World War II. Kennedy's political career began almost immediately after his return from the war. In 1946, he became a member of the U.S. House of Representatives. In 1952, he became a member of the U.S. Senate. After winning the 1960 presidential election, Kennedy was sworn in as the thirty-fifth president of the United States in January 1961. He was 45—the youngest president in U.S. history.

Kennedy's assassination on November 22, 1963, shocked the world. Many people can recall exactly where they were when they learned of the assassination. Kennedy addressed many major events and issues during his short time as president, including the Berlin Wall, the Bay of Pigs, the space race, the Cuban Missile Crisis, the Vietnam War, and the civil rights movement.

Analysts claim that part of Kennedy's success was due to his brilliant use of the media, particularly television. He became an icon for a new beginning for the country. Today, decades after his death, Kennedy is still held in high regard as a president.

taking off around the clock to add to the number normally in the air. By the end of October 23, the U.S. Navy had taken a position 800 miles (1,287 km) from Cuba. U.S. government orders were to intercept any Soviet vessel, if necessary, by force that would disable but not sink it.

TAKING POSITIONS

Kennedy had issued a public ultimatum. In response, Khrushchev sent a confidential letter to the president warning of the catastrophic consequences to world peace if the situation were allowed to escalate. Kennedy pulled the quarantine line to 500 miles (805 km) off the Cuban coast. This gave Khrushchev one more day to decide what to do before Soviet ships would reach the line.

Soviet submarines moved into Caribbean waters and awaited orders. The military forces of Soviet allies were placed on alert. Castro mobilized Cuban troops in preparation for a U.S. invasion.

President Kennedy ordered DEFCON 2, the highest military readiness ever reached during the Cold War. Key West, Florida, located less than 100 miles (161 km) from Cuba, experienced a mass exodus. Across the United States, people shopped for survival goods. They also prayed. The United States and the Soviet Union were ready to battle. The world waited anxiously for what would happen next. ⌐

DEFCON

DEFCON is short for *def*-ense readiness *cond*ition of the U.S. armed forces. There are five levels. Each DEFCON level puts into effect a certain prescribed protocol:
• DEFCON 5:
Usual peacetime military conditions
• DEFCON 4:
National security measures are increased
• DEFCON 3:
Force readiness is increased to more than normal
• DEFCON 2:
Force readiness is increased to just below maximum readiness
• DEFCON 1:
Maximum readiness, declared when attack is imminent or happening
The DEFCON system was put into place after the development of atomic weapons. DEFCON 1 has never been issued. DEFCON 2 has only been issued once, during the Cuban Missile Crisis.

President Kennedy made a national television speech on October 22, 1962, about a naval blockade of Cuba.

0   621 miles (1,000 km)

- Warsaw Pact
- NATO
- Non-aligned

N

Sweden

Norway   Finland

Soviet Union

Denmark

Ireland
United
Kingdom   The Netherlands

East
Germany   Poland

Belgium   West
Germany   Czechoslovakia

Luxembourg

France   Switzerland   Austria   Hungary

Yugoslavia   Romania

Italy   Bulgaria

Spain   Albania

Portugal   Greece   Turkey

Cyprus

Africa   Middle East

*This map shows the division of Europe following World War II,
before the Cuban Missile Crisis.*

EUROPE DIVIDED

he standoff between the Soviet Union and
the United States over Cuba was preceded
by a rivalry that started toward the end of World
War I, in 1917. During the Russian Revolution, the
Bolsheviks overthrew Russia's leader. This started

the Russian Civil War (1918–1921). The war was fought between the Bolshevik Red Army and a loose alliance of anti-Bolshevik forces known as the White Russians. Fearful that Bolshevism might overrun Europe and Asia, countries such as France, England, Japan, Canada, and the United States supported the White Army. This support was not enough. The White Army conceded defeat. The Bolsheviks established the Soviet Union in 1924 as the first communist state. It would become the model for all communist states formed.

WORLD WAR II

During World War II (1939–1945), the United States and the Soviet Union became uneasy allies against Germany. Although they both fought Germany from 1941 to 1945, each country feared that the other might leave the war and settle separately with Adolf Hitler, Germany's leader. Soviet distrust of the West was rooted in the appeasement policy of the Munich Pact in 1938. In the pact, England and France allowed Hitler to annex parts of Czechoslovakia. The Western allies were wary of the Soviet Union because of the Nazi-Soviet Pact of 1939. As a result of this pact, Hitler invaded Poland with the Soviet promise that it would not interfere with the invasion.

The United States and the Soviet Union remained allies only long enough to defeat Germany and Japan. The end of World War II returned the two countries to their previous relationship.

Capitalism and Communism

Developed during the Industrial Revolution, capitalism is a social system of individual rights to the ownership and control of economic resources. In capitalist systems, most means of production are owned privately, by individuals or corporations, and operated to gain a profit. Capitalism is a market economy.

Communism is an economic and political philosophy that emerged from Marxism, a philosophy developed by Karl Marx in the middle of the nineteenth century. Communism attempts to abolish the distinction between rich and poor, and between workers and bosses. There is little or no private ownership of the means of production—natural resources, agriculture, industry, businesses. Government central planning controls most trade and production.

An international movement from its inception, communism became well known throughout the world after the Russian Revolution and the formation of the Soviet Union in 1924. At this time, Russia became the first country to enter the interim stage of the working class rule that Marx described as necessary for communism to occur. Lenin's Bolshevik Party changed its name to Communist Party to distinguish itself from other socialist movements. For the next seven decades, the Communist Party would rule the Soviet Union.

POTSDAM CONFERENCE

From July 17 through August 2, 1945, Joseph Stalin, Winston Churchill, and Harry S. Truman met in Potsdam, Germany, to discuss Germany and postwar

Europe. Stalin, head of the Communist Party, represented the Soviet Union. Prime Minister Churchill represented Great Britain. President Truman represented the United States. Opinions differed greatly over issues of European security and stability. The Soviet Union had been hardest hit by the war. Stalin favored total disarmament of Germany and foreign occupation. He requested war reparations that would effectively dismantle what was left of the German economy. Churchill and Truman favored a democratic organization of Europe as envisioned by the Marshall Plan, with an economically strong and politically healthy Germany at its center.

The men agreed that Germany would be disarmed and divided into four sectors, each supervised by one of the four allies: Great Britain, France, the United States, and the Soviet Union. Germany's capital, Berlin, located in the heart of the Soviet sector, would also be divided into four sectors.

World War II

While World War II started with Hitler's invasion of Poland on September 1, 1939, the countries that would later be considered the major Allied Forces entered the war at different times. The United Kingdom and France declared war on September 3, 1939, honoring their treaties with Poland. The Soviet Union joined the Allies after Hitler's forces attacked the Soviet Union on June 22, 1941. The United States entered the war after Japan, Germany's ally, attacked Pearl Harbor, Hawaii, on December 7, 1941.

British Prime Minister Winston Churchill, U.S. President Harry S. Truman, and Soviet Premier Joseph Stalin pose at the Potsdam Conference.

LONDON CONFERENCE

Between February and June 1948, representatives from the United Kingdom, France, Belgium, the Netherlands, Luxembourg, and the United States met repeatedly to plan for a fusion of the three western zones of occupied Germany into one federal German state. The countries wanted the new

German state to be economically integrated into Europe and to participate in the Marshall Plan. On June 7, 1948, the London Conference announced that a currency reform and a West German constitution were in preparation.

The Soviet Union was not part of the conference. The shaky alliance between East and West had fallen apart. The Cold War had begun.

BERLIN BLOCKADE

The Soviet response to the London Conference came on June 24, 1948. Citing the fusion of the three Western zones as a breach of the Potsdam Agreement, the Soviet Union cut off all rail and road routes going through Soviet territory. Berlin was cut off from the West. The Soviet message was clear: the West should change its policies regarding Germany or leave Berlin—even the Western sectors—altogether.

George C. Marshall

The Marshall Plan is named after its architect, General George C. Marshall. He was the Army chief of staff during World War II under President Roosevelt and the secretary of state under President Truman. Marshall introduced his plan for the recovery of Europe during a 1947 speech at Harvard University. When the Soviet Union refused to let the Eastern Bloc countries participate in the plan, the Marshall Plan was introduced only in Western Europe. As a result of the Marshall Plan, Western Europe quickly rebuilt and modernized its economy, eventually becoming a major trading partner with the United States. In 1948, Marshall was *Time* magazine's Man of the Year. He received the Nobel Peace Prize in 1953.

The West did neither. On June 25, the first U.S. planes were ordered to fly over the Soviet zone, carrying supplies into West Berlin. The Berlin airlift lasted 462 days and involved planes from many Western countries. France helped by building Berlin Tegel, an airport large enough to accommodate the countless planes that flew over Berlin for more than a year.

The Soviet plan backfired. The Western alliance grew stronger. On April 4, 1949, the United States and several other Western countries founded the North Atlantic Treaty Organization (NATO). One of NATO's major principles holds that an attack on any member would result in military action from all NATO members. The founding of NATO was a message to the Soviet Union to proceed with caution.

Berlin Airlift

The Berlin Airlift was a major accomplishment. Countless flights were necessary to supply the entire population of West Berlin with survival goods for more than 15 months. At times, planes landed at the Berlin Tegel Airport as often as one per minute.

The Soviet Union responded by forming the Warsaw Pact, Eastern Europe's counterpart to NATO.

Europe had been divided into two. The division was symbolized by Germany's split into East and West, which was made official in 1949. This division was made even more apparent by the Berlin Wall.

THE BERLIN WALL

West Berlin continued to be a problem for the Soviet Union. Located in the heart of East Germany, it was an open door to the West that allowed East Germans to enter West Germany. Under the Marshall Plan, West Germany had developed a healthy democracy and a fast-growing economy in the 1950s. East Germany had become one of the richest and most advanced countries in the Eastern Bloc. Still, many of its citizens looked to the wealthier West for personal political freedom and individual economic prosperity.

To stop East Germans from going to West Germany, East German leader Walter Ulbricht conceived the idea of the Berlin Wall. Nikita Khrushchev had become premier of the Soviet Union in 1958. Under the condition that the wall would first be nothing but barbed wire that could be dismantled if the West threatened military action, Khrushchev approved the plan in 1961.

On August 13, 1961, construction of the wall began, isolating West Berlin in East German territory.

Fearing that the Cold War might worsen over Berlin, the West, including the United States under newly elected President John F. Kennedy, stood by with little more than verbal protests.

The Soviet Union achieved a small victory, but the results were not entirely positive. While the wall was successful in keeping East Germans from fleeing to West Germany, it became a symbol of Communist tyranny. Still, the Soviet Union continued to move forward. The struggle between East and West grew.

West Berliners, right, watched East German construction workers erect the Berlin Wall in August 1961.

Korea and Vietnam became sites for proxy wars between the Soviet Union and the United States.

Proxy Wars

The struggles between East and West extended beyond Europe via proxy wars. Conflict between the two powers was limited to countries outside their borders, though the wars were actually battles between the superpowers.

THE KOREAN WAR

Following the unconditional surrender of Japan at the end of World War II, the Allies divided Korea along an imaginary line at 38° north latitude. The Soviet Union occupied the North; the United States occupied the South. In 1949, U.S. and Soviet forces withdrew from Korea after setting up governments favoring their respective ideologies. The division set the stage for a civil war, which erupted in 1950.

With Soviet backing, North Korea invaded South Korea on June 25 in an attempt to reunite the country. Within three days, North Korea occupied Seoul, South Korea's capital. In July, President Truman sent U.S. troops to intervene. By September, they had driven the North Koreans back to the dividing line along the thirty-eighth parallel.

In early October 1950, the United States went beyond its policy of containment by attempting to create a united democratic Korea by conquering North Korea. China, a communist state, feared a capitalist

Containment

The policy of containment dates back to the medieval tactic of imposing a siege on the castle of a powerful lord, effectively imprisoning him in his own home. Without supplies and access to his military forces, the lord was rendered helpless and eventually forced to surrender. The primary goal of containment during the Cold War was to prevent the growth of communism beyond the Iron Curtain. The hope was that this would lead to stagnation and eventually to the downfall of the Soviet Empire.

stronghold in Korea and a possible U.S. advance into China. In late October, Chinese forces entered the war in support of North Korea. Chinese and U.S. forces would fight for the next two years. A cease-fire agreement reinstated the borders between North Korea and South Korea. The agreement also established the demilitarized zone around the thirty-eighth parallel.

Both East and West strengthened their alliances. The Soviet Union and China were on one side of the Iron Curtain. The United States, Japan, and the

Proxy War

A proxy war is a conflict in which two powers fight each other using third parties. A third party may be the government of another country, guerilla groups, or terrorist organizations. A pure proxy war is virtually impossible, as the third party often develops its own agenda.

The most notable example is the Israeli-Palestinian conflict, which served as a proxy for hostilities between the Soviet Union and the United States during the Cold War. The Soviet Union supported the Palestinian Liberation Organization and the United States supported Israel; however, the issues at the heart of the conflict go beyond communism and capitalism. The conflict continuously erupts over sovereignty in the land of Israel/Palestine. Jewish leaders claim a historical connection to the area as their ancestors had lived in Palestine before the Diaspora, in which Jews dispersed to areas outside of Palestine. The Arab people of Palestine feel that a Jewish state is a violation of Arab historical rights in the region and makes an independent Palestine state impossible.

The United States did not immediately support Israel in the Arab-Israeli war of 1948. However, when the Soviet Union supported the Arab attack against Israel, the United States put its resources behind Israel.

Western allies were on the other. The Korean War made the Cold War a worldwide confrontation.

THE VIETNAM WAR

After decades of French rule, Vietnam, led by communist Ho Chi Minh, fought for independence. In 1954, the French left Vietnam. The country was divided into North and South along the seventeenth parallel. North Vietnam was placed under the communist rule of Ho Chi Minh. South Vietnam was noncommunist under Dgo Dinh Diem.

U.S. foreign policy at the time was based on the "domino theory." In this theory, the fall of South Vietnam to communism would lead to the fall of the rest of Southeast Asia to communism. The U.S. government anticipated that Soviet power might then spread beyond Southeast Asia. Vietnam became a primary battlefield in the Cold War.

Starting in 1954, U.S. military trainers and advisors went to South Vietnam to help Prime Minister Diem face opposition from guerilla forces sympathizing with North Vietnam.

Demilitarized Zone

The border between North Korea and South Korea is the most heavily guarded border in the world. Approximately 1 million soldiers stand guard on the two sides of the inappropriately named "demilitarized zone," an area 155 miles (249 km) long and 2.5 miles (4 km) wide that cuts across the thirty-eighth parallel.

Khrushchev encouraged North Vietnam to reunite the country under Ho Chi Minh in a Communist state.

On August 1, 1962, Kennedy signed the Foreign Assistance Act, providing "military assistance to countries which are on the rim of the Communist world and under direct attack."[1] The law paved the way for direct U.S. military intervention in Vietnam.

The animosity between the United States and the Soviet Union that started after World War II continued to grow. The division of Europe, Korea, and Vietnam increased pressures for each superpower to show strength against the opponent. Another battle was on the horizon. This time, the countries would face each other over Cuba.

Kennedy's Inaugural Address

John F. Kennedy's famous inauguration speech on January 20, 1961, comments on communist aggression in general and North Vietnam in particular. In his speech, Kennedy said, "We shall pay any price, bear any burden, meet any hardship, support any friend, oppose any foe to assure the survival and the success of liberty."[2] A year later, during his State of the Union Address on January 11, 1962, Kennedy reiterated his tough political stance on containment, saying, "Few generations in all of history have been granted the role of being the great defender of freedom in its maximum hour of danger."[3]

U.S. Special Forces trained South Vietnamese fighters in July 1962.

*Cuban refugees prayed for the success of the Bay of Pigs invasion
at a rally in Miami, Florida.*

CUBA AS A PAWN

C uba was a Spanish colony until the
Spanish-American War in 1898.
During the war, the United States fought for Cuba's
independence. The Spanish were defeated quickly.
Cuba was freed from Spanish rule, but the United
States occupied the country for four years. The Platt

Amendment of 1901 granted Cuba self-government under U.S. supervision of the country's foreign relations. The United States was also granted the right to intervene militarily if U.S. security became threatened. To that effect, the United States established a permanent naval base at Guantanamo Bay, Cuba. President Theodore Roosevelt granted Cuba full independence in 1902.

While under Spanish rule, Cuba was an agricultural country economically dependent on its sugar, tobacco, and coffee plantations. As a Spanish colony, Cuba exported mainly to Europe. After the Spanish-American War, U.S. companies bought Cuban land and invested in sugar. By the mid-1920s, the United States controlled almost two-thirds of the Cuban sugar industry. Most of Cuba's crops were exported to the United States. Economically, Cuba was dependent on the United States. This allowed the United States to exert control over the country.

BATISTA'S RISE TO POWER

After a series of military coups, Fulgencio Batista rose to power in the 1930s. He became president of Cuba in 1940. He was voted out of office in 1944, but he maintained power behind the scenes. Batista became president again in 1952 after staging a coup.

Batista suspended constitutional rights, held rigged elections, and persecuted those opposed to him with police scare tactics. His regime was characterized by the influence of foreign investors, mainly from the United States. The United States owned hotels and casinos that lured tourists to the island, especially to Havana—Cuba's capital. The American Mafia took hold of most of the gambling industry—corruption ran rampant.

Most of the population did not share in the wealth. Batista's government became unpopular. The middle class, students, and the rural population wanted change.

The Cuban Revolution

From 1956 to 1959, revolutionaries led by Fidel Castro

"I warn you, I am just beginning! If there is in your hearts a vestige of love for your country, love for humanity, love for justice, listen carefully ... I know that the regime will try to suppress the truth by all possible means; I know that there will be a conspiracy to bury me in oblivion. But my voice will not be stifled—it will rise from my breast even when I feel most alone, and my heart will give it all the fire that callous cowards deny it. ... Condemn me. It does not matter. History will absolve me."[1]

—*Fidel Castro, October 16, 1953, during his trial by the Batista regime*

fought a guerilla war against the Batista government. On January 1, 1959, Castro's rebel army took Havana. Batista fled the country. Castro became Cuba's leader.

Most of Cuba's population celebrated Castro. He and his revolutionary comrade, Che Guevara, enjoyed folk hero status the world over.

Castro wanted to improve the living conditions of all Cubans and gain true independence from U.S. economic influence. He closed down the gambling industry and forced out the American Mafia. He nationalized many U.S. companies, making them state-owned Cuban property. Castro cut rents in half and then changed them into mortgages. Thousands of urban Cubans now became homeowners. He initiated a rural land reform that limited the amount of land one individual could own. Foreign-held land was given

Ernesto Che Guevara

One of the most revered icons of any international socialist movement was Ernesto Che Guevara. An Argentinean Marxist, Guevara joined Fidel Castro's "26th of July Movement" in Mexico. He became one of the most influential Cuban rebel leaders and later held various posts in Castro's government. In 1965, Guevara left Cuba to join rebel forces in Bolivia. He was captured by the CIA and turned over to Bolivian authorities. Guevara was executed by the Bolivian army in 1967. A photograph of Guevara taken by Alberto Korda and turned into pop art by Andy Warhol has perpetuated Che Guevara's fame long after his death.

to Cuban peasants. Castro brought health care and education to rural areas. All of these measures were meant to redistribute Cuba's wealth and break down old class barriers. Castro inspired pride and solidarity among many citizens.

Among the middle class, however, Castro's support declined. This group was hit hard by his economic reforms and disappointed by his refusal to hold elections. Many middle-class Cubans lost the jobs they had held with U.S. companies and income from rental properties.

Fidel Castro

Fidel Alejandro Castro Ruz was born on August 13, 1926, on a Cuban sugar plantation. Upon graduating from a Catholic boarding school, Castro enrolled in law school at the University of Havana. The university was a center for the political and social uprisings at the time. Castro was attracted to the promise of socialism to do away with class distinctions and to distribute wealth more evenly.

After graduating in 1950, Castro practiced law, representing the poor and underprivileged. After Batista's military coup in 1952, Castro abandoned his law practice and went underground to plot against Batista's regime and run for the country's House of Representatives. Almost half of Castro's rebel army died in a failed attack on July 26, 1953. Most of the survivors, including Castro and his brother, Raul, were eventually captured and sentenced to life in prison. In 1955, Batista issued a general amnesty to show confidence in the popularity of his government. Fidel and Raul Castro reunited with other Cuban rebels in Mexico, formed the "26th of July Movement" to commemorate the failed first attack against Batista, and returned to Cuba. From 1956 through January 1, 1959, Castro led a guerilla war against Batista. On January 9, 1959, Castro marched into Havana. On February 16, 1959, he was sworn into office as prime minister of Cuba.

Like Batista, Castro did not treat his opponents kindly, imprisoning many and executing some. Consequently, many anti-Castro Cubans left for the United States, settled in Florida, and formed a very vocal anti-Castro lobby that criticized him as a communist dictator.

THE U.S. EMBARGO

Once Castro took over Cuba, relations between Cuba and the United States quickly soured. On April 15, 1959, Castro visited Washington, D.C., but President Eisenhower refused to meet him.

Over the next few years, relations between the two countries deteriorated into low-level warfare. Castro's seizures of U.S. investments prompted increasing U.S. economic sanctions. By the end of 1960, Eisenhower had restricted U.S. purchases of Cuban sugar, limited oil trade, and prohibited all exports to Cuba. In response, Castro seized the assets of many U.S. businesses in Cuba, often with little or no compensation to the owners. With the economic security of his country threatened, Castro turned to the Soviet Union for support. The Soviet Union became Cuba's main trading partner. The United States was losing influence over Cuba.

Cuba's economic alignment with the Soviet Union increased U.S. distrust of Castro. Despite his public assurances that Cuba was neutral in the Cold War, the United States feared that Cuba would soon be a base of communism in the Western hemisphere. This would threaten the stability of Latin America. Eisenhower broke off diplomatic relations with Cuba in January 1961, two weeks before President Kennedy's inauguration.

THE BAY OF PIGS INVASION

Kennedy inherited a shaky relationship with Castro. The seriousness of the rift became evident when Kennedy learned of secret plans to overthrow Castro. The CIA was planning to support an invasion of Cuba by those who had left the country disillusioned by Castro's revolution and settled mainly in Florida. The plan rested on the belief that the Cuban population would rise against Castro and aid the invaders. When Kennedy took office, the CIA had been training the exiled Cubans for months. On April 14, the exile army landed on the southern coast of Cuba at the Bay of Pigs.

The invasion was a disaster. The army was trapped in swampland, unable to advance, and easily defeated by Castro's army. Approximately 1,300 invaders were killed or taken prisoner. The Cuban population did not rise against Castro. Instead, citizens supported him fervently. Kennedy was under great pressure to send U.S. military support. He not only refused to get involved, he denied that the United States had participated in the disaster.

Cuba and the rest of world knew better. Castro publicly denounced U.S. imperialism and officially declared himself a communist. The Bay of Pigs was an international disaster for the United States.

THE CUBA PROJECT

Fearful that Cuba could start a rapid spread of communism throughout Latin America, the CIA devised other plans to overthrow Castro. On November 3, 1961, Kennedy authorized aggressive covert operations that came to be known as the Cuba Project or Operation Mongoose. Plans included tapping

Bay of Pigs Invasion

The Bay of Pigs invasion occurred April 17 through April 19, 1961. Organized by the CIA, 1,400 armed Cuban exiles landed at the Bay of Pigs on the southern coast of Cuba on April 17. The exiles were met by Cuban military forces: 20,000 troops on land and bombers overhead. The small group of exiles was no match for such forces. By the time the attack was over on April 19, more than 100 exiles had been killed, almost 1,200 had surrendered, and others escaped. Those who were taken prisoner were held for 20 months. After much negotiation, Kennedy was able to free the prisoners in exchange for $53 million in baby food and drugs given to Castro.

CIA Operations

The Central Intelligence Agency (CIA) is part of the U.S. government. The CIA gathers and analyzes information about foreign governments, corporations, and persons. The CIA uses this information for propaganda or public relations purposes. If necessary, for national interests or security, the CIA may release false information to the public. The CIA engages in covert operations to preserve U.S. interests abroad and U.S. security at home. The president has to authorize all such covert operations. Project Cuba (Operation Mongoose) and Operation Ortsac are only two examples of the CIA's covert work. The question of whether covert CIA operations are legal, moral, and effective has caused much debate.

into and fueling anti-Castro sentiment among the population and destroying sugar crops. Except for blowing up several bridges and burning down a few sugar fields, the Cuban Project was never fully executed. By that time, plans had changed as a result of unexpected developments.

Castro was aware of CIA activities in Cuba and fearful that the animosities with the United States might escalate into a full-blown invasion. Castro turned to the Soviet Union for help. In early 1962, Khrushchev realized the need to defend the only communist state in the Western hemisphere and decided to install nuclear missiles on the island.

The Cuban Missile Crisis was about to begin.

Fidel Castro, February 26, 1957

Senator Joseph McCarthy's anticommunist campaign resulted in one of the worst waves of censorship in the United States.

THE COLD WAR AT HOME

he Cold War guided U.S. foreign policy. The Truman Doctrine and the Marshall Plan were designed to rebuild Western Europe after the devastation of World War II. They were also intended to contain communism behind the

Iron Curtain. Although the United States and its allies had won World War II, awareness of Soviet military might and concerns that the U.S. economy would return to the grim conditions of the 1930s were sources of anxiety for many Americans. The use of nuclear weapons in 1945 and the first Soviet explosion of an atomic bomb in 1949 further increased feelings of unease, even though U.S. military might was second to none and the U.S. economy continued to grow.

Anticommunist sentiments were an essential part of the U.S. mindset. The 1949 clash with the Soviet Union over Germany, China's fall to the Maoists in the same year, and the beginning of the Korean War made the Cold War the focus of U.S. fears and hatred. This atmosphere paved the way for Senator Joseph McCarthy's aggressive anticommunist campaign.

McCarthyism

Joseph McCarthy's influence resulted in one of the worst waves of censorship the United States has experienced. More than 300 books were banned. The mere suspicion of being a sympathizer of communism or liberal philosophies could easily result in being blacklisted, investigated, or persecuted. Blacklisting is putting names of people on a list to be punished or denied privilege in some way. An anticommunist hysteria swept the nation in the 1950s that resulted in deliberate harassment of people with uncommon or less-than-popular views, particularly in terms of politics. This reaction and behavior became known as McCarthyism.

Although McCarthy's allegations could never be substantiated, he received widespread support among Americans. Many politicians, including Senator John F. Kennedy, did not speak out against McCarthy for fear they might lose voters.

McCarthy was elected to the U.S. Senate from Wisconsin in 1946. He gained notoriety in 1950 when he claimed to have a list of Communist Party members and Soviet spies employed by the U.S. State Department. His accusations fell on a receptive audience. The House Un-American Activities Committee had just convicted Alger Hiss, a State Department official, of espionage. McCarthy gained enough support in the U.S. Senate to launch a massive investigation into the State Department. Through government bodies such as the Senate Internal Security Committee and the Senate Permanent Subcommittee on Investigations, McCarthy conducted dozens of investigations of alleged communist infiltrations of the U.S. government and the U.S. military between 1950 and 1954.

Investigation into the supposed communist infiltration of the U.S.

military eventually caused McCarthy's downfall. Broadcast on national television, McCarthy's tactics and rhetoric bordering on verbal abuse eventually eroded his credibility. On December 2, 1954, the Senate voted to condemn the investigations based on an examination of McCarthy's methods, rendering him powerless.

THE 1960 PRESIDENTIAL CAMPAIGN

Fear of communism continued throughout the 1950s. The 1960 U.S. presidential campaign and election between Republican Vice President Richard Nixon and Democratic Senator John F. Kennedy were strongly influenced by issues of the Cold War.

On May 1, 1960, a U.S. spy plane was shot down over Soviet air space. The United States first denied allegations of espionage. When the Soviet Union produced the pilot, the plane, and the film showing

McCarthy's Downfall

Joseph McCarthy's downfall was aided by his appearance on *See It Now,* Edward R. Murrow's television news report. By analyzing McCarthy's speeches, showing discrepancies and false claims, *See It Now* criticized McCarthy for overrating the nationwide fear of communists. McCarthy's rebuttal on the show proved just as damaging. Not knowing how to use the power of television to his advantage, McCarthy came across as a fierce and unforgiving persecutor. His public support diminished quickly.

footage of Soviet military installations, President Eisenhower accepted responsibility. He also implied that such missions would continue. Khrushchev demanded an apology for the invasion of Soviet airspace. When none came, diplomatic relations between Eisenhower and Khrushchev deteriorated. Khrushchev broke off the Paris summit for East-West relations scheduled for mid-May.

During the presidential election campaign, candidates Nixon and Kennedy evoked the fear of world communism. Kennedy claimed that an apology to Khrushchev by the Eisenhower administration might have saved the Paris summit. This played into the Republican claim that Democrats were soft on communism. Nixon likened Kennedy's call for an apology to Franklin Roosevelt's policy of appeasement toward Hitler in the Munich Agreement, which gave part of Czechoslovakia to Germany. Nixon claimed that Kennedy was the kind of man "Mr. Khrushchev would make mincemeat of."[1] Nixon presented himself as a man who would always stand up to Khrushchev.

Kennedy's rebuttal criticized the Eisenhower-Nixon administration for allowing the United States to slip behind the Soviet Union economically and militarily. At that time, the economic growth rate of the Soviet Union was higher than that of the United States. However, Kennedy's claim that the Soviet Union had more missiles could not be substantiated. Nonetheless, many Americans were receptive to Kennedy's claims. This was due in part to the clearly superior Soviet space program— yet another area where the United States was behind the enemy. The Soviets had successfully launched several satellites beginning in 1957.

"We Will Bury You"

At a Moscow reception in 1956, Nikita Khrushchev reportedly stunned Western ambassadors by saying, "Whether you like it or not, history is on our side. We will bury you."[2] Some political commentators interpreted this as a warning of future aggression against the United States. Others interpreted it as his expression of confidence in his country's bright future because its economy grew more rapidly than the U.S. economy during the 1950s. The U.S. media condemned Khrushchev's comment and applauded the ambassadors who left the room in outrage.

Khrushchev had a reputation for undiplomatic behavior. He often interrupted and frequently insulted speakers—sometimes purposefully and sometimes not. During a United Nations debate on October 13, 1960, he took off one of his shoes and banged it on his desk to underline his words of anger against a Philippine delegate who had criticized the Soviet Union for taking over Eastern Europe.

Khrushchev's erratic behavior and often careless word choices received much media attention. Many historical analysts argue that Khrushchev's loss of support within the Politburo, the Communist Party's executive committee, in 1964 had as much to do with his unsophisticated behavior as with the winds of political change.

Fidel Castro, left, and Nikita Khrushchev met on the floor of the United Nations General Assembly in New York on September 20, 1960.

Soviet confidence was high. Khrushchev claimed that communism would survive if a war were to occur. The growing relationship between Khrushchev and Castro increased U.S. anxiety over communist superiority. Castro was portrayed as Khrushchev's man in Havana. Fear that other

Latin American countries might fall under Soviet influence fueled the worry over Cuba's relationship with the Soviet Union.

Cuba became a campaign issue. Kennedy accused the Eisenhower-Nixon administration of losing Cuba to the Soviet Union through its economic policies that forced Castro into an economic relationship with Khrushchev. He held the current administration responsible for the perceived encroachment of communism in the Western hemisphere.

The Cold War politics during the 1960 presidential campaign created a powerful momentum for Kennedy. His rhetoric during the campaign fed Americans' fear of communism. Long before the Soviet missiles were discovered in Cuba, Kennedy found himself under pressure to show U.S. strength and resolve. The slightest appearance of weakness might prompt memories of appeasement policies during World War II. Kennedy's lack of forcefulness in response to the building of the Berlin Wall may have been considered a sign of weakness. However, Americans did not think Kennedy a weak candidate. To the contrary, Kennedy was elected president in 1960.

In his inaugural address on January 20, 1961, Kennedy promised to defend freedom "in its hour of maximum danger."[3] Kennedy had no choice but to pursue hard-line politics. He would stand up to Khrushchev to the brink of nuclear war.

The Impact of Television

Television was relatively new in the 1950s. Politicians and public figures had not yet learned to use its power to their advantage. They relied more on words than appearance. Historical analysts claim that Richard Nixon lost the 1960 presidential election mainly because he did not come across well on television. Kennedy, however, came across very well on television.

President Kennedy delivered his inaugural address on January 20, 1961.

Hiroshima, Japan, after the atomic bomb was dropped

THE ARMS RACE

On August 6, 1945, the United States dropped "Little Boy" over Hiroshima, Japan. Three days later, the United States detonated "Fat Boy" over Nagasaki, Japan. The two atomic bombs caused massive destruction and almost

200,000 deaths, mostly civilians. The attacks prompted Japan's surrender in World War II. However, the devastation caused by the bombs did not end with the war. Nuclear fallout caused even more civilian deaths for many years.

The devastation and death caused by these two bombs created an international outcry demanding a ban of nuclear weapons. The deteriorating relationship between the United States and the Soviet Union after World War II made both superpowers reluctant to accept any limitations on their nuclear weapons programs. The U.S. Atomic Energy Commission was formed in January 1946 to further develop weapons of mass destruction.

The Soviet Union launched its own nuclear weapons program in an effort to catch up with the United States. On August 29, 1949, the first successful Soviet nuclear test

The Manhattan Project

In 1939, President Franklin D. Roosevelt received a letter from Albert Einstein warning that Adolf Hitler was developing a bomb of unprecedented destructive power using nuclear fission. The Manhattan Project was born. The project was a joint endeavor of the United States and Great Britain aimed at developing nuclear weapons to be used against Nazi Germany. But by the time the first atomic bomb was tested in July 1945, Germany had already surrendered. The bomb was never used against Hitler.

was conducted. Aware that the Soviet Union was now a nuclear power as well, President Truman authorized tests for the development of the hydrogen bomb, or H-bomb. An H-bomb was potentially hundreds of times more powerful than the atomic bombs dropped in Japan. The arms race had begun.

Mutual Assured Destruction

Containment had been a major principle of the Truman Doctrine, which held that communism had to be stopped at the Iron Curtain in defense of the free world. Containment was to be achieved by the policy of deterrence due to the threat of massive retaliation. The development of nuclear weapons gave this military strategy a new dimension. Planning for the use of nuclear weapons soon became an integral part of the official U.S. policy of containment.

Once nuclear weapons were developed, deterrence rested on mutual assured destruction (MAD). MAD was a fact of life after the Soviets had the capacity to strike the continental United States with enough nuclear weapons to cause millions of casualties. Once MAD was attained, each side could deter a nuclear attack on its own territory by its opponent. MAD implied that neither side would dare to strike first because the other side would surely have struck back with equal or greater force, resulting in the annihilation of both nations. The suicidal aspect of a first strike was believed to guarantee a tense, but stable, peace. Both nations tried to gain a military advantage that would make the threat of a disarming first strike credible.

While MAD may have prevented a major confrontation between the two superpowers, it also may

MAD and Popular Culture

The doctrine of MAD made its way into popular culture rather quickly. *MAD Magazine*—particularly its black-and-white *Spy versus Spy* comic strip—depicts the futility of a continued arms race to ensure peace.

Stanley Kubrick's *Dr. Strangelove or How I Learned to Stop Worrying and Love the Bomb* is a 1964 movie satirizing MAD. After a nuclear first strike on the Soviet Union is launched by a renegade bomber commander, the president of the United States desperately tries to avoid a nuclear catastrophe.

Dr. Seuss's *The Butter Battle Book* is a rhyming antiwar story published in 1984. It depicts the logic of MAD when a deadly confrontation over the correct way to butter bread threatens to escalate into war.

have diverted armed combat to a series of proxy wars. MAD also kept the arms race alive and active. Each side was determined to amass enough nuclear weapons to destroy the other.

THE SOVIET SPUTNIK PROGRAM

By the mid-1950s, bombs became smaller and lighter. The delivery systems—the planes, submarines, and missiles that would carry the bombs to the point of detonation—could travel farther and faster. Nuclear warheads became small enough to be used in land mines and in air-to-air missiles carried by jet fighters. For example, the U.S. B-52 jet bomber was designed specifically to penetrate Soviet airspace. This seemed to give the United States a considerable advantage. The United States could deliver the bombs to places where they could cause the most damage to the Soviet Union. In 1957, however, this advantage began to erode.

On October 4, 1957, the Soviet Union launched *Sputnik I*, the world's first artificial satellite. It was clear that if the Soviet Union had missiles that could deliver a satellite into space, the same missile could carry a nuclear bomb a very long distance to a U.S. target.

This first official picture of the Soviet satellite Sputnik I
was issued in Moscow on October 9, 1957.

America's confidence was shattered. The
Soviet Union appeared to be ahead in the space
program and in the arms race. Khrushchev's
constant predictions that history would favor
communism over capitalism seemed to be coming
true. Khrushchev was named Man of the Year in

1957 by *Time* magazine. The top secret *Gaither Report* issued a warning that the Soviet Union's economic focus on military development could lead to "a threat which may become critical in 1959 or early 1960."[1] The arms race had been refueled.

Eisenhower was less concerned about a possible short-term Soviet advantage. He knew that in the long run, U.S. missiles would be numerous and in hardened silos or on submarines. They also would become more accurate.

Working Around the Clock

From midnight on October 20 to midnight on October 22, 1962, the U.S. State Department worked nonstop to inform diplomatic corps members and world leaders of the Cuban Missile Crisis. The State Department:

- Sent the president's speech and a letter from the president to Khrushchev to the U.S. embassy in Moscow and to the Soviet ambassador in Washington, D.C.
- Sent a letter from the president to the leaders of 21 Latin American countries, Britain, Canada, France, India, and the mayor of West Berlin.
- Dispatched high-level briefing officers to Britain, France, and West Germany.
- Provided oral briefings to journalists and 95 foreign ambassadors.
- Sent the president's speech to 129 embassies and consulates.
- Sent instructions to 60 U.S. embassies regarding the president's speech.
- Informed U.S. embassies in Latin America of the U.S. call for an Organization of American States (OAS) and supplied text for a proposed OAS resolution.
- Delivered a letter to the U.N. Security Council president calling for an urgent meeting that included a draft resolution.
- Sent a draft of the Security Council resolution to 21 Latin American countries.

JUPITER MISSILES IN TURKEY

In 1959, Turkey agreed to host a U.S. missile site. Similar missile sites had already been established in Great Britain and Italy. At the end of 1960, the United States launched a Jupiter missile near Izmir, Turkey. The Jupiter was a ballistic missile that could travel 1,500 miles (2,414 km) in only 16 minutes. It could easily reach cities in the western part of the Soviet Union, including its capital, Moscow. If equipped with nuclear warheads, the Jupiter missiles could become very destructive.

Khrushchev protested the deployment of nuclear missiles in Turkey. While there were several U.S. missile sites in Europe, the site in Turkey was aimed at Moscow. At the time, the Soviet Union did not have any missiles stationed where they could have threatened the United States directly. The Cuban missiles detected on October 14, 1962—the first Soviet missile sites outside the Soviet Union—were positioned to counter the Jupiter missiles in Turkey.

The Soviet Union could destroy U.S. cities. Should these missiles be fired, the United States would have little warning. In as few as five

"Bombs do not choose. They will hit everything."[2]
—*Nikita Khrushchev Moscow Rally, August 12, 1961*

"I look forward to a great future for America—a future in which our country will match its military strength with our moral restraint, its wealth with our wisdom, its power with our purpose."[3]

—John F. Kennedy, Remarks at Amherst College, October 26, 1963

minutes, U.S. decision makers would have to determine if reports of an attack were genuine and, if genuine, how to respond. But the Cuban missiles did not upset the overall balance in the arms race. The logic of MAD still held. Each side threatened the other with retaliation—all the way to the brink of nuclear war.

Nikita Khrushchev, April 1956

Kennedy sat at his desk in the White House on October 23, 1962, shortly after signing a presidential proclamation concerning Cuba.

THE CRISIS DEEPENS

At 10:00 a.m. on October 24, 1962, the U.S. quarantine of Cuba officially took effect. Two Soviet ships and a Soviet submarine were within miles of the quarantine line. The U.S. Navy had orders to force the submarine to the surface if it did not stop at the line. U.S. commanders had been instructed to avoid hostilities. However, Secretary of Defense Robert McNamara explained during the Ex-Comm meeting that morning that the United States must expect and prepare for hostilities.

At 10:25 a.m., the message arrived that the Soviet ships had stopped in the water. Secretary of State Dean Rusk reportedly announced, "We're eyeball to eyeball, and I think the other fellow just blinked."[1]

Whether Khrushchev blinked by ordering Soviet vessels not to cross the quarantine line or whether Kennedy blinked by pulling back the quarantine line may be subject to debate. The reality is that on the early morning of October 24, 1962, both sides stood still. This provided an opportunity for U.N. Secretary General U Thant to open diplomatic channels.

A Diplomatic Impasse

At the request of more than 40 U.N. member states, U Thant sent identical messages to Kennedy and Khrushchev at 2:00 p.m. on October 24. He urged the men to avoid nuclear war at all cost.

"Let us never negotiate out of fear. But let us never fear to negotiate."[2]
—John F. Kennedy,
Inaugural Address,
January 20, 1961

U.N. Secretary General U Thant

U Thant suggested suspending both the quarantine and the Soviet arms shipments while trying to find a diplomatic solution to the crisis.

Between 9:25 p.m. and 1:45 a.m., Khrushchev and Kennedy exchanged letters, each man holding the other responsible for the crisis. Khrushchev believed the crisis had been provoked by the quarantine, an act of aggression by the United States. He demanded that the quarantine be removed and the Soviet ships be allowed to pass. Kennedy reminded Khrushchev of the premier's repeated assurances that no offensive missiles would ever be placed in Cuba and that breaking that promise had initiated the crisis. Kennedy's letter repeated the demand to remove the missiles to avoid an escalation of the crisis.

On the afternoon of October 25, Kennedy responded to U Thant's proposal. However, he did not address the suggestion to suspend the quarantine. Based on information that work on the Cuban missile sites had not slowed, Kennedy feared that lifting the quarantine temporarily might give the Soviet Union enough time to finish the missile sites and make them fully operational.

Stevenson versus Zorin

On October 25, 1962, the U.N. Security Council held an emergency session to discuss the Cuban Missile Crisis. Adlai Stevenson, the U.S. ambassador to the United Nations, demanded that the Soviet representative, Valerian Zorin, admit that offensive missiles were stationed in Cuba. Fed up with the Soviet ambassador's evasiveness, Stevenson said, "Don't wait for the translation, answer 'yes' or 'no.'"[3] When Zorin refused to respond to Stevenson's interrogation style, Stevenson uttered, "I am prepared to wait for your answer until Hell freezes over."[4] When still no answer came, Stevenson proceeded to show the photographs that proved the presence of the missile sites. Stevenson had always been a gifted speaker, yet his confrontation with Zorin was probably the most significant political coup of his career.

Kennedy considered removing the missiles in Turkey as a trade. The U.S. ambassador in Turkey warned that Turkey would deeply resent any such bargain because removal would mean weakening protection of a friend to appease a foe. There seemed to be no diplomatic solution.

BACK-CHANNEL COMMUNICATIONS

On the afternoon of October 26, Aleksander Fomin, the Soviet Embassy's public affairs counselor, met with John Scali, an *ABC News* correspondent. The two men had lunch together every month. On this day, Fomin had an important message. The Soviet Union was willing to remove the Cuban missiles in exchange for a guarantee from the United States never to invade Cuba. Fomin offered a way out of the official impasse.

Back-channel Diplomacy

Back-channel diplomacy refers to the unofficial communication between governments. Such communications often deal with issues of political sensitivity that cannot be discussed in the spotlight of public opinion because they may not align with set policies.

At 6:00 p.m., a private letter from Khrushchev arrived at the U.S. State Department. In an emotional appeal not to let the situation escalate, Khrushchev offered what Fomin had relayed earlier. The Soviet Union would remove the Cuban missiles in exchange for a public non-invasion pledge by the United States. A peaceful resolution to the crisis seemed within reach. However, the worst was yet to come.

BLACK SATURDAY

Castro was fearful that a U.S. invasion of Cuba was imminent. He spent the evening of October 26, 1962, in the Soviet Embassy in Cuba in a bomb shelter. He cabled Moscow for help, arguing that a U.S. invasion of Cuba could be prevented only by a preemptive strike. Castro told Khrushchev to use his missiles or risk losing them to the United States. Castro's belligerent stance seemed realistic considering that the members of the U.S. Joint Chiefs of Staff were drawing up invasion plans.

At 6:00 a.m. on Saturday, October 27, the CIA reported that several Cuban missile sites were fully operational. The mobilization of traditional Cuban military forces was in full swing.

John Scali

As an intermediary during the Cuban Missile Crisis, *ABC News* reporter John Scali played an important role in the event by taking a critical Soviet message about settling the crisis to U.S. officials. Scali's involvement in politics continued. In 1971, he served as a foreign affairs advisor to President Richard Nixon. In 1973, he became U.S. ambassador to the United Nations. Scali returned to ABC in 1975. He worked there until 1993, when he retired. John Scali died on October 9, 1995, at the age of 77.

At 9:00 a.m., Radio Moscow broadcast an official message from Khrushchev. The message was more antagonistic than his private letter from the night before. Khrushchev now demanded the removal of the missiles in Turkey before the Cuban missiles could be dismantled. Ex-Comm feared that Khrushchev might have lost power to others in the government who wanted strict adherence to Soviet policy and were unwilling to compromise with the United States.

Kennedy reconsidered his options for dealing with the situation. He was convinced that the quarantine alone would not solve the missile issue. He also felt that a missile exchange might not be a viable course of action. Kennedy decided to go with the third option by giving the order to prepare for an air strike against the missile sites and an invasion of Cuba the following Monday. He also ordered the U.S. Defense Department to create two plans for civil defense: one in response to an armed conflict with conventional weapons and one in response to nuclear war.

At 10:15 a.m., a U.S. U-2 plane supposedly became lost due to a navigation mistake and flew into Soviet airspace. The aircraft left Soviet airspace

On October 23, 1962, Castro replied to Kennedy's naval blockade via Cuban radio and television.

before Soviet interceptors could shoot it, but the situation only worsened.

At noon, a U.S. reconnaissance plane was shot down over Cuba, killing its pilot, Major Rudolf Anderson. Files made public long after the Cuban Missile Crisis reveal that the order to open fire on U.S. spy planes had come from local Soviet commanders, not Khrushchev. At the time, Ex-Comm assumed that the attack order had come from Moscow. The Soviets had fired the first shot. The rules of engagement required paying back in kind.

Kennedy refused to authorize immediate retaliatory action. Instead, he requested that Khrushchev's demand to trade the Cuban missiles for the Turkish missiles be discussed further. Gradually, the idea emerged to ignore the Radio Moscow transmission and respond only to Khrushchev's letter. The letter had not requested the removal of the Turkish missiles, only a public promise never to invade Cuba. Ex-Comm members feared that any trade with the Soviet Union might severely damage the NATO alliance. The Joint Chiefs of Staff insisted on the air strike and invasion planned for Monday—just two days away.

We Are Going to War

In a more private meeting, President Kennedy, Attorney General Kennedy, Secretary of State Rusk, Secretary of Defense McNamara, and National Security Advisor Bundy agreed unanimously to accept Khrushchev's original offer. Robert Kennedy was selected to offer the deal to show that it had the full support of the president.

On the evening of October 27, Attorney General Kennedy and Soviet Ambassador Dobrynin met at the Soviet embassy. Kennedy's message was that the United States would give a public non-invasion pledge if the Cuban missiles were removed. The deal also included the private assurance that the Jupiter missiles in Turkey would be removed. This part of the deal was to remain secret; the Jupiter missiles would be removed later and gradually so that the connection to Cuba would not be obvious. Kennedy demanded an answer within 24 hours. If the Soviets did not respond by that time, the United States would be forced to go to war on Monday morning.

Castro's Letter to Khrushchev

Fearing U.S. attack, Castro appealed to Khrushchev for help in a letter dated October 26, 1962, writing:

[I] consider an attack to be almost imminent—within the next 24 to 72 hours. There are two possible variants: the first ... is an air attack against certain objectives with the limited aim of destroying them; the second ... is a full invasion. ...

... the imperialists invade Cuba ... the dangers of their aggressive policy are so great that after such an invasion the Soviet Union must never allow circumstances in which the imperialists could carry out a nuclear first strike against it. ...

I believe that the imperialists' aggressiveness makes them extremely dangerous, and that if they manage to carry out an invasion of Cuba ... then that would be the moment to eliminate this danger forever, in an act of the most legitimate self-defense. However harsh and terrible the solution, there would be no other. ...

The imperialists, without regard for world opinion and against laws and principles, have blockaded the seas, violated our air-space, and are preparing to invade, while ... blocking any possibility of negotiation. ...

We wish you success with the enormous task and great responsibilities which are in your hands.[2]

At 9:00 a.m. on Sunday, October 28, 1962, Radio Moscow transmitted Khrushchev's message. The Cuban missiles would be dismantled. In a private letter to Khrushchev, President Kennedy stated that both governments should promptly carry out their promises. There was still concern that the concession to remove the Jupiter missiles from Turkey would cause the president's political downfall. That portion of the agreement was kept secret even from members of Ex-Comm.

At 1:00 p.m., Khrushchev's order to dismantle the Soviet missiles was sent to Cuba. Disassembly began at 5:00 p.m. that day. Secretary of Defense McNamara ordered the Jupiter missiles removed from Turkey by April 1 of the following year.

The Cuban Missile Crisis was over. The world breathed a sigh of relief. ⌒

A Soviet ship carried eight canvas-covered missiles and transporters, visible on decks, away from Cuba on November 7, 1962.

*A U.S. destroyer intercepted a Russian freighter
on November 10, 1962, to inspect cargo.*

LOOKING BACK

The manner in which the Cuban Missile
Crisis was resolved has been the subject of
much debate. The resolution did not find approval
everywhere. Castro was not consulted in the final
dealings between the United States and the Soviet

Union. He felt betrayed by the Soviet Union and Khrushchev.

TAKING A STAND

Standing up to the other side was extremely important to both superpowers. It seemed impossible for either side to publicly back down without hurting its image. The Cuban Missile Crisis supported the policy of brinkmanship, the notion that if you stand tough you win. It also supported policies of crisis management designed to avoid actions that would provoke the other side into using force.

Immediately following the Cuban Missile Crisis, Kennedy's public hard-line politics earned him the opposing labels of brilliant and reckless. He had pushed Khrushchev to the brink by issuing a public ultimatum and backing it up with the quarantine. Some considered this evidence of a strong leader who was willing to defend democracy by any means. In the face of maximum danger, Kennedy emerged victorious.

After the Crisis

The Cuban Missile Crisis ended on October 28, 1962, but it took several months before the actions agreed to in the crisis negotiations were completed. The U.S. blockade ended November 20. The Soviet missiles were removed from Cuba by the end of 1962. The U.S. Jupiter missiles in Turkey were removed in 1963.

Soviet Premier Khrushchev, left, and U.S. President Kennedy

Others criticized Kennedy for risking nuclear
war unnecessarily by arguing that there was no
maximum danger because the Cuban missiles
were no real threat to U.S. military supremacy.
Kennedy stood firm in an effort to keep Cuba from
becoming a major Soviet military base. Not doing

so could have made him appear weak in the eyes of voters. This might have jeopardized his political career. In addition, some members of Kennedy's administration thought he would have faced impeachment, or removal from office, if he had not acted.

Khrushchev's role in the Cuban Missile Crisis also has been met with differing judgments. Some people criticized Khrushchev's deployment of missiles in Cuba as simply military one-upmanship. These critics fault him for underestimating U.S. determination. Complying with the ultimatum and dismantling the missiles is evidence of a weak politician who backed down when met with resistance. Others have argued that missiles were stationed in Cuba for good reason. They countered the Jupiter missiles in Turkey and could defend Cuban independence following the Bay of Pigs invasion and other CIA operations aimed at Castro. Khrushchev's compliance with the ultimatum was a willingness to sacrifice his personal political career rather than risk an all-out war with the United States and a nuclear catastrophe.

"The more bombers, the less room for doves of peace."[1]
—Nikita Khrushchev, Moscow Radio, March 14, 1958

It was not until the 1969 publication of *Thirteen Days*, Robert Kennedy's memoir, that a more complex analysis of the crisis became public. Neither President Kennedy's firm stance nor Premier Khrushchev's concessions resolved the crisis. The crisis was resolved with diplomacy. U.N. Secretary General U Thant's intervention diffused the situation by calling for an alternative to hard-line politics. Meetings between Fomin and Scali paved the way for letters

Nikita Khrushchev

Nikita Khrushchev was born on April 17, 1894, in a town on the Russian-Ukraine border. His parents were peasants who could not read. Khrushchev probably could not read until his teenage years. His family moved to a more urban area in 1908, and he began working in a factory. His activism began in a union protesting working conditions. He fought with the Red Army during the Russian Revolution. In 1918, he joined the Bolshevik Party, which later became the Communist Party.

After the formation of the Soviet Union, he worked his way up through the party ranks in Kiev. His career soared. After Stalin died in 1953, Khrushchev eventually became the new leader of the Communist Party of the Soviet Union and the true leader of the Politburo.

In 1958, he became the Premier of the Soviet Union. Like Kennedy, Khrushchev signaled a new beginning. While in office, he promoted economic change and denounced the excesses of terror under Stalin. Despite the crises with the West, he was the first Soviet leader to actively promote peaceful coexistence and a friendly competition between the two superpowers. His policy was based on his belief in the superiority of communism. He believed that the Soviet Union would prevail. In 1964, he was ousted by conservative Communists and succeeded by Leonid Brezhnev. Khrushchev died on September 11, 1971.

between Kennedy and Khrushchev that discussed a diplomatic solution. Lastly, the meeting between Robert Kennedy and Anatoly Dobrynin, sanctioned by President Kennedy and Premier Khrushchev, finalized the deal: Cuban missiles in exchange for a public nonaggression guarantee issued by the United States and a secret exchange of Cuban for Turkish missiles.

Khrushchev's willingness to accept the secrecy of the missile exchange made the Cuban Missile Crisis resolution a success for the United States. Secretary of State Rusk later claimed that President Kennedy was willing to offer an official and public trade through the United Nations rather than declare war on that Monday if the crisis had not been resolved by the secret meeting between Robert Kennedy and Dobrynin. While it might be true that Khrushchev blinked by

Thirteen Days

Thirteen Days is the title of Robert Kennedy's memoir of the Cuban Missile Crisis and the title of a movie released in 2000. The movie provides a succinct history lesson and effectively captures the tense Ex-Comm meetings that often were characterized by a clash of opinions between the Joint Chiefs of Staff and President Kennedy. While taking some dramatic license, the movie draws heavily on the once-secret White House tapes of the Ex-Comm meetings.

not insisting on a public and official missile trade, Kennedy was just as willing to blink. Neither man wanted to go to war. Both men acted as would any statesman faced with such an important moment in history: they reacted to the pressures of the time.

Robert F. Kennedy

*A Polaris missile was fired from a nuclear submarine
at Cape Canaveral, Florida, on July 20, 1960.*

BEYOND THE CRISIS

The Cuban Missile Crisis brought the world closer to a nuclear catastrophe than had ever been experienced. Immediately after the crisis, negotiations resumed to limit the nuclear arms race. Nuclear arms control had first been demanded immediately after the bombings of Nagasaki and Hiroshima. However, negotiations had been inconsistent, depending on the relationship between the two superpowers. The Partial Test Ban Treaty was signed by 113 nations in August 1963. The treaty limited nuclear tests to under water and outer space to ensure that nuclear fallout would not contaminate the planet. Test ban treaties were considered a major step toward nuclear disarmament. The most immediate result of the crisis was the installation of a hotline between Moscow and Washington, D.C., that improved communication capabilities between the Soviet Union and the United States.

The Treaty on the Non-proliferation of Nuclear Weapons followed in July 1968. It prohibited all nations that did not have nuclear weapons from acquiring or developing them, and it required those with nuclear weapons to begin taking steps toward nuclear disarmament. Signed by 188 nations, the treaty was the beginning of many treaties designed to limit the threat of nuclear war. From 1969 through 1991, U.S. and Soviet leaders met and signed several arms control agreements. Initial negotiations became known as Strategic Arms Limitation Talks (SALT). Later negotiations were called Strategic

Arms Reduction Treaty (START). There were also negotiations on banning nuclear weapons in outer space and on the seabed, as well as the reduction of conventional forces in Europe.

The Cold War ended in 1991 with the collapse of the Soviet Union. However, this did not bring an end to the issue of nuclear weapons. The threat of nuclear attack still exists. Concern over the possession of nuclear weapons has shifted to the Middle East and South Asia.

In September 1996, the Comprehensive Test Ban Treaty was adopted by the United Nations and signed by 71 nations. The treaty includes provisions for a comprehensive international monitoring system. In the years since the treaty was signed, more than 100 additional countries have joined the ban. However, as of early 2007, Korea, India, and Pakistan had not signed the treaty. China, Iran, Israel, and the United States had signed the treaty but had not ratified it. The United States believes the proposed monitoring process is not effective enough and is concerned about the effects of the treaty on the U.S. stockpile of nuclear weapons. The United States strongly supports banning nuclear weapons in countries that do not yet have nuclear capabilities.

At the same time, the United States insists on maintaining its own nuclear stockpile as a deterrent in case monitoring processes falter and defiant nations develop or obtain nuclear arms. The logic of MAD, though now directed toward the Middle East and Southeast Asia, still exists.

THE COLD WAR AFTER CUBA

The policy of brinkmanship had consequences for the remainder of the Cold War. Publicly, each side blamed the other for the Cold War. In 1964, Leonid Brezhnev took power in

Open Communication

The importance of open communication between superpower leaders became evident during the Cuban Missile Crisis. The 12 hours it took to receive, decode, and verify Khrushchev's initial letter to Kennedy allowed too much time for misunderstandings. It took so much time that Khrushchev's official address came over Radio Moscow by the time Kennedy was ready to respond to Khrushchev's second letter.

In August 1963, the two superpowers signed an agreement to establish a hotline that would link the White House to the Kremlin, Russia's seat of government. The hotline is a teletype located in the Pentagon, the National Military Command Center, with a link to the Situation Room in the basement of the White House. The hotline relies on the written word rather than voice or video transmission. This allows for time to think before responding and to avoid the potential misinterpretation in tone of voice and body language. The hotline was used several times during the Cold War.

The hotline is still in operation and tested daily. The Pentagon sends a test message every even hour. Moscow sends a message back every odd hour. The test messages are not political. They are recipes or literary excerpts that cordially test the translation skills of the operator on the other side.

the Soviet Union. Khrushchev had lost support
in the Kremlin, partly because of his handling
of the Cuban Missile Crisis. Brezhnev's policy
of safeguarding communism in the Eastern Bloc
provided justification for military intervention in
Czechoslovakia in 1968. Economic reforms and
political liberalization in the country had stirred
fears that Czechoslovakia might leave the Warsaw
Pact. On August 20, 1968, the Soviet Union invaded
the country and arrested its leader.

The United States was engaged in safeguarding
its interests as well. During the Vietnam War
(1964–1973), the United States was engaged in
a vicious guerilla battle with the Viet Cong, the
South Vietnamese communist militia supported
by communist North Vietnam. The massive
military engagement met increasing criticism by
Americans. The United States began to hand over
combat responsibilities to the South Vietnamese.
The Paris Peace Accords of January 1973 officially
accepted both North Vietnam and South Vietnam as
independent nations. The United States withdrew
military support from South Vietnam. In 1975,
North Vietnam took over South Vietnam. The
countries were reunited as the Socialist Republic of

Vietnam on July 7, 1976. The war was
a costly and humiliating defeat for
the United States.

The 1970s was a period of
détente, or easing of tensions,
between the United States and the
Soviet Union. German Chancellor
Willy Brandt initiated a policy of
reconciliation between West Germany
and East Germany.

In 1972, President Richard
Nixon went to Moscow to sign the
SALT I agreements. He also visited China to initiate
trade contacts and normalize relations that had
been troubled since the Maoists had taken control
in 1949. In 1979, the United States and China
established formal diplomatic relations. That same
year, President Jimmy Carter and Soviet Premier
Leonid Brezhnev signed SALT II.

However, on December 24, 1979, only six
months after signing SALT II, the Soviet Union
invaded Afghanistan to keep its communist
government in place. The United States spoke out
against the invasion, leading a 64-nation boycott
of the 1980 Summer Olympic Games in Moscow.

Jimmy Carter, left, and Leonid Brezhnev signed the SALT II treaty in 1979.

President Carter halted sales of American grain to the Soviet Union, but Ronald Reagan resumed them when he became president.

Détente was over, and a period of intense reawakening of the Cold War followed in the 1980s. Reagan revived the ideological competition of the Cold War. Despite prior treaties to limit weapons of mass destruction, he increased military spending. The increase included funding for his Strategic Defense Initiative (SDI), an attempt to develop weapons systems to shoot down missiles in mid-flight. Although only partially successful, SDI provided defensive capabilities that seemed to make winning a nuclear war possible.

The United States also engaged in additional proxy wars with the Soviet Union. The United States supported anticommunist forces in Nicaragua, Lebanon, and Afghanistan.

Soviet Collapse

The war in Afghanistan became a major factor in the collapse of the Soviet Empire. Dubbed the "Soviet Vietnam," the guerilla war lasted a decade. President Carter gave aid to Afghan guerillas partly with the idea of provoking Soviet intervention. The war drained the Soviet economy. In 1985, Mikhail Gorbachev became the leader of the Soviet Union. His policy of *Perestroika*, or mass initiative, prescribed rapid economic reforms. The Soviet Union would move away from state ownership and central planning toward local initiatives and private ownership. The policy of *glasnost* followed with political reforms, relaxed censorship, and an encouragement of public debate. The media quickly exposed the Soviet Union's economic problems and political corruption. Faith in the Soviet system waned. The Soviet Union was slowly losing its grip on the East. In 1988, the Soviet Union declared that it would no longer intervene in the affairs of other Eastern Bloc countries.

The Soviet Empire ended in 1989. The Soviet Union withdrew from Afghanistan. That year, the first free elections were held in Poland. Lech Walesa, leader of the liberal labor movement Solidarity that had taken hold in Poland in 1980, won the election. Solidarity's success sparked a series of peaceful revolutions in other Eastern Bloc countries.

The borders to the West opened. Hungary removed its border restrictions to Austria on August 23, 1989. Thousands of East German tourists made their way to Austria through Hungary. Czechoslovakia allowed the stream of East German refugees to cross its borders. Mass demonstrations against the East German leadership led to the resignation of Erich Honecker, East Germany's leader, on October 18. On November 9, the borders between East Germany and West Germany opened. That night, thousands of people climbed the Berlin Wall, chipping at it with bare hands, hammers, and champagne bottles. The symbol of a world divided into East and West had fallen—peacefully. The Cold War was over.

FIDEL CASTRO

Much has changed in the world in the years since the Cuban Missile Crisis. Leaders on both sides of the conflict have come and gone. Khrushchev has been followed by Brezhnev and a handful of other leaders. Kennedy has been succeeded by eight U.S. presidents. Castro has outlasted them all.

Castro's image has evolved over time. During the 1950s and 1960s, he went from romantic revolutionary to ruthless dictator. During the 1970s, he became the political underdog who withstood the antagonism of a superpower. During the 1980s, Castro was considered a

"General Secretary Gorbachev, if you seek peace, if you seek prosperity for the Soviet Union and Eastern Europe, if you seek liberalization: Come here to this gate! Mr. Gorbachev, open this gate! Mr. Gorbachev, tear down this wall!"[1]

—*Ronald Reagan, Remarks at the Brandenburg Gate, West Berlin, Germany, June 12, 1987*

leader of the developing world. During the 1990s, his continued confrontation with the United States and his ever-present anti-American rhetoric prompted critics to write him off. They described him as a relic of an era that has long since passed, stubbornly unwilling to harness the economic possibilities of a better relationship with the United States.

Cuba's future does not lie with Castro due to his advanced age. In July 2006, Castro, almost 80 years old, temporarily transferred all duties to his younger brother, Raul. Yet, his political vision may influence Cuba for decades to come. There are young Castro supporters in important government positions, and Cuba's growing relationships with the European Union and China allow continued independence from the United States. Perhaps one day Cuba and the Unites States will come together and reconcile. Just as it did during those tense days of the Cuban Missile Crisis in October 1962, the world will have to wait and see. ⌐

The Cold War Ends

The Cold War was officially declared over at the Malta summit meeting between Soviet Premier Mikhail Gorbachev and U.S. President George H.W. Bush in December 1989. At the time, the meeting was hailed as the most important summit meeting since 1945. In that year, Winston Churchill, Joseph Stalin, and Theodore Roosevelt first discussed postwar Europe in Yalta.

Castro addressed a crowd of tens of thousands in Bayamo, Cuba, on July 26, 2006.

TIMELINE

1959	1960	1961
Castro takes over Havana on January 1 and is sworn in as Cuba's leader on February 16.	Cuba aligns with the Soviet Union economically.	The Bay of Pigs attack in April does not remove Castro from power and is a complete failure for the United States.

1962	1962	1962
On October 21, Kennedy asks the press for 24 hours of secrecy.	Kennedy addresses the nation on October 22, issuing an ultimatum to Khrushchev to remove the Cuban missiles.	DEFCON 3 is issued on October 22. The U.S. Navy takes position at the quarantine line in Caribbean waters.

1962

1962

1962

Soviet Ambassador Gromyko assures Kennedy on October 18 that there are no offensive weapons in Cuba.

On October 19, Ex-Comm prepares options for dealing with the missiles; the U.S. State Department prepares civil defense measures.

On October 20, Kennedy sets in motion a quarantine of weapons to Cuba.

1962

1962

1962

The quarantine takes effect on October 24 at 10:00 a.m.

Soviet vessels stop or turn around on October 24 at 10:25 a.m.

At 2:00 p.m. on October 24, U.N. General Secretary U Thant urges Kennedy and Khrushchev to seek diplomatic solutions.

TIMELINE

1962

1962

1962

1962

Between 9:25 p.m., October 24, and 1:45 a.m., October 25, Khrushchev and Kennedy exchange letters.

On October 25, Kennedy all but rejects U Thant's suggestion to suspend the quarantine and to open negotiations with Khrushchev.

Fomin and Scali open back-channel communications on October 26.

1962

1962

1962

On October 27, Castro cables Khrushchev for help in case of an invasion.

At 9:00 a.m. on October 27, Radio Moscow delivers Khrushchev's demand to remove the missiles in Turkey.

A U.S. plane is shot down in Cuban air space at noon on October 27, killing the pilot.

1962

At 6:00 p.m. on October 26, Khrushchev's private letter to Kennedy reiterates Fomin's back-channel offer.

1962

Castro spends the evening of October 26 in a bomb shelter at the Soviet Embassy.

1962

At 6:00 a.m. on October 27, CIA reports several missile sites fully operational.

1962

Attorney General Kennedy and Soviet Ambassador Dobrynin meet on the evening of October 27 to discuss a deal.

1962

On October 28, at 9:00 a.m., Radio Moscow delivers Khrushchev's pledge to remove the missiles in exchange for a U.S. non-invasion pledge.

1962

On October 28, at 1:00 p.m., Khrushchev orders the removal of the Soviet missiles in Cuba, ending the crisis.

ESSENTIAL FACTS

DATE OF EVENT

October 14–28, 1962

PLACE OF EVENT

Cuba, Caribbean Sea, White House, Kremlin

KEY PLAYERS

❖ John F. Kennedy, president of the United States

❖ The Executive Committee of the Security Council of the United States (Ex-Comm)

❖ Nikita Khrushchev, premier of the Soviet Union

❖ Fidel Castro, president of Cuba

❖ U Thant, secretary-general of the United Nations

HIGHLIGHTS OF EVENT

❖ In fall of 1962, the Soviet Union established missiles in Cuba capable of carrying nuclear weapons to virtually any U.S. city.

❖ Reconnaissance flights over Cuba detected the missiles on October 14, 1962.

❖ President Kennedy and Ex-Comm, a group of military and political advisors, discussed possible reactions, ranging from diplomacy to an all-out invasion of Cuba.

❖ President Kennedy issued an ultimatum to Soviet Premier Khrushchev on national television on October 22, 1962. The Soviet Union was to remove the missiles or provoke a military confrontation that might escalate into nuclear war.

❖ The United States imposed a quarantine on Cuba on October 24, 1962, which did not allow Soviet vessels carrying military cargo to pass.

❖ President Kennedy and Premier Khrushchev exchanged letters discussing possible deals that might resolve the crisis in nonmilitary ways.

❖ The conflict was resolved by the exchange of the Cuban missiles for a public non-invasion guarantee and secret removal of U.S. Jupiter missiles in Turkey months later.

QUOTE

"I call upon Chairman Khrushchev to halt and eliminate this clandestine, reckless and provocative threat to world peace and to stable relations between our two nations. I call upon him further to abandon this course of world domination, and to join in an historic effort to end the perilous arms race and to transform the history of man. He has an opportunity now to move the world back from the abyss of destruction—by returning to his government's own words that it had no need to station missiles outside its own territory, and withdrawing these weapons from Cuba—by refraining from any action which will widen or deepen the present crisis—and then by participating in a search for peaceful and permanent solutions."—*President John F. Kennedy, Address to the Nation, October 22, 1962*

ADDITIONAL RESOURCES

SELECT BIBLIOGRAPHY

Chang, Laurence, and Peter Kornbluth, eds. *The Cuban Missile Crisis 1962. A National Security Archive Documents Reader*. New York: The New Press, 1998.

Frankel, Max. *High Noon in the Cold War: Kennedy, Khrushchev and the Cuban Missile Crisis*. New York: Ballantine Books, 2004.

George, Alice. *Awaiting Armageddon*. Chapel Hill, NC: University of North Carolina Press, 2003.

Lansdale, Edward. *Operation Mongoose: The Cuba Project*. 20 Feb. 1962. Cuban History Archive (2000). <http://www.marxists.org./history/cuba/subject/cia/mongoose/c-project.htm>.

Weisbrot, Robert. *Maximum Danger: Kennedy, the Missiles and the Crisis of American Confidence*. Chicago: Ivan Dee, 2001.

FURTHER READING

Brugioni, Dino. *Eyeball to Eyeball*. New York: Random House, 1990.

Chrisp, Peter. *The Cuban Missile Crisis*. Milwaukee, WI: World Almanac Library, 2002.

Miroff, Bruce. *Pragmatic Illusions: The Presidential Politics of John F. Kennedy*. New York: David McKay Company, 1976.

Preble, Christopher. *John F. Kennedy and the Missile Gap*. DeKalb, IL: Northern Illinois University Press, 2004.

Stern, Sheldon. *Averting "The Final Failure": John F. Kennedy and the Secret Cuban Missile Crisis Meetings*. Stanford, CA: Stanford University Press, 2003.

Walton, Richard. *Cold War and Counter-Revolution: The Foreign Policy of John F. Kennedy*. New York: Viking Press, 1972.

Web Links

To learn more about the Cuban Missile Crisis, visit
ABDO Publishing Company on the World Wide Web at
www.abdopublishing.com. Web sites about the Cuban Missile
Crisis are featured on our Book Links page. These links are
routinely monitored and updated to provide the most current
information available.

Places To Visit

Berlin Wall Documentation Center
Bernauer Strasse III, 13355 Berlin, Germany
++49 (0)30 / 464 10 30
www.berliner-mauer-verein.de/index_e.html
The center has information about the history of the Berlin wall.
The center is one facet of a memorial site that includes the Berlin
Wall Memorial and the Chapel of Reconciliation.

The John F. Kennedy Presidential Library and Museum
Columbia Point, Boston, MA 02125
866-JFK-1960, 617-514-1600
www.jfklibrary.org
Dedicated to the memory of John F. Kennedy, the museum
portrays his life, leadership, and legacy.

**The National Atomic Museum (National Museum of Nuclear
Science and History)**
1905 Mountain Road Northwest, Albuquerque, NM 87104
505-245-2137
www.atomicmuseum.com
Established in 1969, museum exhibits include the Manhattan
Project, World War II, the Cold War, and a history of arms control.

Glossary

appeasement
> The policy or act of allowing rather than opposing the actions of an aggressor.

arms race
> The struggle between two or more countries for military superiority.

capitalism
> An economic system in which the means of production are privately owned and it is governed by the principles of a free market economy: supply and demand.

Cold War
> The period between 1945 and 1989 that was characterized by a conflict between the Soviet-led East and the United States-led West over ideological differences.

communism
> An ideology pursuing a classless society based on the common ownership of the means of production.

containment
> The U.S. foreign policy during the Cold War, it was meant to stop the influence and spread of the Soviet Union and communism.

coup
> The taking over of a government illegally and with violence.

covert
> Secret, clandestine, unofficial.

détente
> French for "ease" and "relax," this term was used to describe the more relaxed relationship between the United States and the Soviet Union in the 1970s.

deterrence
> A military strategy that holds that threatening an opponent with a massive retaliatory strike if attacked will deter the opponent from attacking.

Iron Curtain

> The border that divided Europe into the Eastern Bloc and the Western Bloc. The Berlin Wall was considered the physical representation of the division.

mutual assured destruction (MAD)

> A military strategy in which the suicidal aspect of striking first is meant to deter both sides from actually striking first.

Politburo

> Short for Political Buro, the executive committee of the Communist Party of the Soviet Union.

protocol

> An established process for dealing with a particular kind of situation.

proxy war

> A war not fought by the principal opponents but by third parties.

reconnaissance

> The active gathering of information about an enemy.

reparation

> Compensation for war damages paid by a nation defeated in war.

sanctions

> Actions taken by one country to make another country act in a certain way.

surveillance

> The passive gathering of information about someone or something by monitoring behavior, events, and actions.

Source Notes

Chapter 1. The Crisis Unfolds
1. John F. Kennedy. Radio and Television Report to the American People on the Soviet Arms Buildup in Cuba. *The White House*. 22 Oct. 1962. <http://www.jfklibrary.org/.>
2. Ibid.

Chapter 2. Europe Divided
None.

Chapter 3. Proxy Wars
1. John F. Kennedy. "314 – Remarks Upon Signing the Foreign Assistance Act." 1 Aug. 1962. *The American Presidency Project*. Ed. Gerhard Peters and John T. Woolley. 2007. 11 Nov. 2007 <http://www.presidency.ucsb.edu/ws/index.php?pid=8797>.
2. John F. Kennedy. Inaugural Address. Washington, DC. 20 Jan. 1961. *The American Presidency Project*. Ed. Gerhard Peters and John T. Woolley. 2007. 11 Nov. 2007 <http://www.presidency.ucsb.edu/ws/index.php?pid=8032>.
3. John F. Kennedy. State of the Union Address. White House, Washington, DC. 11 Jan. 1962. *The American Presidency Project*. Ed. Gerhard Peters and John T. Woolley. 2007. 11 Nov. 2007 <http://www.presidency.ucsb.edu/ws/index.php?pid=9082>.

Chapter 4. Cuba as a Pawn
1. Fidel Castro. History Will Absolve Me. 16 Oct. 1953. Havana, Cuba: Editorial de Ciencias Sociales, 1975. 1997, Castro Internet Archive (marxists.org) 2001. 11 Nov. 2007 <http://www.marxists.org/history/cuba/archive/castro/1953/10/16.htm>.

Chapter 5. The Cold War at Home
1. Robert Weisbrot. *Maximum Danger: Kennedy, the Missiles and the Crisis of American Confidence*. Chicago: Ivan Dee, 2001. 20.
2. *Time*. "We will bury you." 26 Nov. 1956. 2007. 11 Nov. 2007 <http://www.time.com/time/magazine/article/0,9171,867329,00.htm>.
3. John F. Kennedy. Inaugural Address. Washington, DC. 20 Jan. 1961. *The American Presidency Project*. Ed. Gerhard Peters and John T.

Woolley. 2007. 11 Nov. 2007 <http://www.presidency.ucsb.edu/ws/index.php?pid=8032>.

Chapter 6. The Arms Race
1. Security Resources Panel of the Science Advisory Committee. Deterrence and Survival in the Nuclear Age (Gaither Report). Washington: Executive Office of the President, Nov. 1957. 1.
2. Nikita Khrushchev. Moscow rally, Moscow, Russia. 12 Aug. 1961. Bartleby.com. 2005. 11 Nov. 2007 <http://www.bartleby.com/63/90/190.html>.
3. John F. Kennedy. America's Promise and America's Future. Amherst College, Amherst, Massachusetts. 26 Oct. 1963. Peace Corps Online. 11 Nov. 2007 <http://peacecorpsonline.org/messages/messages/2629/2017645.html>.

Chapter 7. The Crisis Deepens
1. Laurence Chang and Peter Kornbluh. Ed. *The Cuban Missile Crisis, 1962. A National Security Archive documents Reader*. New York: The New Press, 1998. National Security Archive, George Washington University. 11 Nov. 2007 <http://www.gwu.edu/~nsarchiv/nsa/cuba_mis_cri/annals.htm>.
2. John F. Kennedy. Inaugural Address. Washington, DC. 20 Jan. 1961. The American Presidency Project. Ed. Gerhard Peters and John T. Woolley. 2007. 11 Nov. 2007 <http://www.presidency.ucsb.edu/ws/index.php?pid=8032>.
3. "Until Hell Freezes Over." *Time*. 2 Nov. 1962. 11 Nov. 2007 <http://www.time.com/time/magazine/article/0,9171,874589,00.html>.
4. Ibid.
5. Fidel Castro. "To Nikita Khrushchev." 26 Oct. 1962. John F. Kennedy Presidential Library and Museum Web site. 11 Nov. 2007 <http://www.jfklibrary.org/jfkl/cmc/cmc_castro_khrushchev.html>.

Chapter 8. Looking Back
1. Nikita Khrushchev. Radio Moscow Address. 14 Mar. 1958. Bartleby.com. 2005. 11 Nov. 2007 < http://www.bartleby.com/63/88/188.html>.

Source Notes Continued

2. John F. Kennedy. Cuban Missile Crisis Address to the Nation. 22 Oct. 1962. White House, Washington, DC. 11 Nov. 2007 <http://www.americanrhetoric.com/speeches/jfkcubanmissilecrisis.html>.

Chapter 9. Beyond the Crisis
1. Ronald Reagan. Remarks at the Brandenburg Gate. 12 June 1987. West Berlin, Germany. 11 Nov. 2007 <http://www.reaganfoundation.org/reagan/speeches/wall.asp>.

INDEX

Index Continued

ABOUT THE AUTHOR

Helga Schier was born in Germany and has a Ph.D. in language and literature. Schier has written and published on a variety of subjects, including art, education, history, language, literature, and social studies. She lives in California with her husband and two children.

PHOTO CREDITS

AP Images, cover, 3, 6, 17, 22, 27, 34, 43, 50, 53, 54, 63, 64, 66, 71, 75, 76, 78, 83, 84, 90, 96, 97, 98, 99; Harvey Georges/AP Images, 10; Red Line Editorial/Nicole Brecke, 18, 28; Horst Faas/AP Images, 33; Herbert K. White/AP Images, 44; TASS/AP Images, 59; Javier Galeano/AP Images, 95